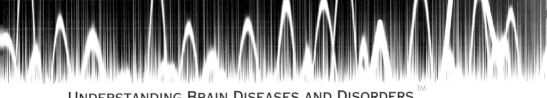

UNDERSTANDING BRAIN DISEASES AND DISORDERS™

BIPOLAR DISORDER

BASIA LEONARD AND JOANN JOVINELLY

ROSEN
PUBLISHING®

New York

Published in 2012 by The Rosen Publishing Group, Inc.
29 East 21st Street, New York, NY 10010

Library of Congress Cataloging-in-Publication Data

Leonard, Basia.
Bipolar disorder/Basia Leonard, Joann Jovinelly.—1st ed.
    p. cm. (Understanding brain diseases and disorders)
Includes bibliographical references and index.
ISBN 978-1-4488-5542-1 (library binding)
1. Manic-depressive illness—Juvenile literature. I. Jovinelly, Joann.
II. Title.
RC516.L46 2010
616.89'5—dc23

                                                          2011021794

Manufactured in China

CPSIA Compliance Information: Batch #W12YA: For further information, contact Rosen Publishing, New York, New York, at
1-800-237-9932.

CONTENTS

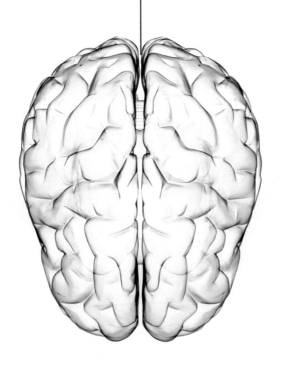

Introduction

Depression has been around since the beginning of human history. It is painful and destructive, and it affects people of all ages, nationalities, religions, and races. United States president Abraham Lincoln was so troubled by depression in the mid-nineteenth century that he described himself as "the most miserable man living."

There are various types of depression. One of the most complex types is bipolar disorder (BD), also known as manic-depressive illness. Bipolar disorder is a condition that causes a person's mood to swing back and forth between two opposite emotional states: depression and mania. In depression, a person has a sad or low mood and is typically inactive and withdrawn. A person in a manic state, on the other hand, has an abnormally elevated mood and is often mentally and physically hyperactive.

People with bipolar disorder go through intense mood changes, feeling extremely happy and excited at times and down and depressed at other times.

These vastly different emotional states are sometimes experienced in isolated phases, or as complex combinations of both depression and mania. The rate and degree to which a person experiences these dramatic emotional changes can vary greatly from person to person.

In the past, depression and bipolar disorder were not considered distinct brain illnesses. Different treatments for each illness did not exist. Today, we know a great deal about how to identify bipolar disorder and how to treat it with medication and psychotherapy. Advanced brain imaging techniques are helping scientists identify the brain structures involved in mood disorders and providing new ways to study the effectiveness of treatments. Scientists are constantly making new discoveries about bipolar disorder, and new medications are being developed and tested all the time. These developments provide hope that more and more individuals with bipolar disorder will be able to lead healthy, productive lives.

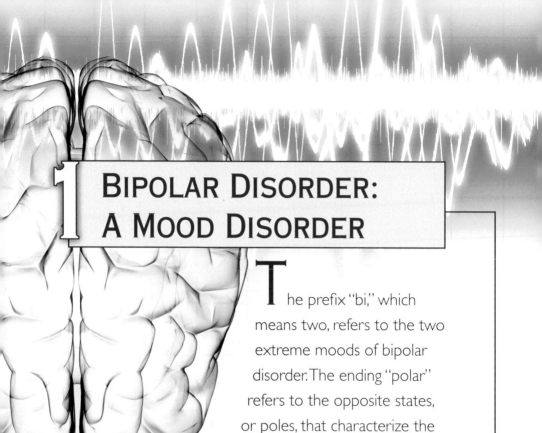

1 BIPOLAR DISORDER: A MOOD DISORDER

The prefix "bi," which means two, refers to the two extreme moods of bipolar disorder. The ending "polar" refers to the opposite states, or poles, that characterize the illness. A person with bipolar disorder suffers from the lows or sadness of depression. The person also experiences mania, which is characterized by extreme enthusiasm and excitement, as well as disorganized thinking and behavior.

Mood Episodes

Someone who suffers from bipolar disorder may have periods of depression, in which he or she feels sad, lonely, weak, and helpless. At other times, the person may have periods of mania, in which he or she feels overly energetic and supremely confi-dent. These different periods are known as mood episodes.

A person's mood might go from low and despairing during a depressive episode to elated and overexcited during a manic episode, and then back to low and despairing again. Because these episodes are so different and are often interspersed with seemingly "normal" periods, bipolar disorder is difficult to diagnose.

To make matters even more complicated, a single mood episode can sometimes include symptoms of both depression and mania. A person with bipolar disorder can also experience irritation, explosive anger, or anxiety during a mood episode.

Depression or Depressive Episodes

The teenage years are filled with many life changes, so it is not uncommon to experience moodiness. As you become more independent, new stressors appear in your life. Some of the issues you are dealing with, like dating and peer pressure, may be confusing.

Instances when you feel sad or down for a brief period are normal, especially while growing up. At these times, you may slam the door to your room and feel like hiding from everyone. You might be angry, irritated, or unreasonably critical of your-self. Sometimes these feelings are reactions to a specific prob-lem, such as a conflict at school or trouble with a friend.

A person who is depressed or experiencing a depressive episode often feels sad and hopeless. She may lose interest and pleasure in most activities.

In addition, as your body changes, the levels of hormones also change, increasing and sometimes disrupting your body chemistry. These chemical imbalances can make you feel stressed, sad, or emotional. This is natural.

However, the low moods that occur in clinical depression and bipolar disorder are different from the normal bad moods that everyone experiences. Depression is more intense, and the low feelings last day after day. Although feelings of sadness can come and go, depression lingers. It can get worse if left untreated by a professional. Depression affects one's emotional state and can leave a person feeling empty or worried, teary or desperate. It also affects a person physically. Depressed people often complain of feeling exhausted. They may experience unexplained headaches, stomach ailments, or back pains.

If you have been in a sad or hopeless state for most of the day, nearly every day, for more than a week or two, you might be suffering from depression or having a depressive episode. Ask yourself the following questions: How extreme is my low mood? How long have I been feeling this way, and how is it interfering with my life? If your low mood has been going on for some time and is making it hard for you to function, you should definitely tell an adult you trust.

Because adults sometimes make the mistake of viewing teens as naturally moody, they may say things like, "You're just going through a difficult phase." If this happens, state clearly how you are feeling. Real problems with depression should not be ignored.

Depression Checklist

Depression is a disease on its own, and it is also one part of bipolar disorder. If you are concerned that you are depressed or that someone close to you is experiencing depression,

Sleep problems, such as sleeping too much or too little, can be a symptom of the depressive phase of bipolar disorder.

consider the following questions. Do you or does someone you know seem to:

- Feel sad and anxious?
- Feel responsible for things that go wrong?
- Get irritated by the slightest problem?
- Tend to overeat or feel unable to eat at all?
- Have no hope for the future?
- Have trouble enjoying things that used to be pleasurable?

- Feel weak or tired?
- Sleep too much or not enough?
- Have little self-control?
- Cut classes, skip meetings and activities, and avoid social events?
- Drink or take drugs, hoping to feel better?
- Find it difficult to concentrate or make decisions?
- Feel out of control?
- Have frequent headaches or backaches?
- Frequently think about or talk about death, suicide, or self-injury?

If you can answer yes to four or more of these questions and you have had these symptoms for several weeks, you might be depressed. If you suspect that a friend or relative is depressed or going through a depressive episode, speak to an adult you trust.

Mania or Manic Episodes

After a depressive period, people who have bipolar disorder will eventually experience feelings of extreme happiness and euphoria. This is the manic phase of the disorder.

Mania is a state of high, unnatural excitement. During a manic episode, a person behaves hyperactively—like he or she has too much energy—for a long period (more than a week or two). During this time, a person feels restless and finds it difficult to calm down or sleep, night after night. The person may have racing thoughts, and his or her speech may be rapid, jumping quickly from one idea to another.

Since a manic person feels as if he or she is overflowing with energy, the emotions of a manic episode may seem pleasurable. Manic feelings can escalate easily, often into states of euphoria.

While feeling high and happy is one sign of mania, symptoms can also include agitation and irritability.

Symptoms of mania often include a decreased desire for sleep, a need for intense activity, and an excessive need to communicate. Other symptoms are varied and may include irresponsible overspending, intense creative phases, and making rash and impulsive decisions. Hypersexuality, or talking and thinking about sex often, is another common symptom.

Hypomania

A milder form of mania is called hypomania. During episodes of hypomania, people feel energized, outgoing, extremely happy, and enthusiastic. However, their energy and activity levels are not as extreme as in mania. Also, the episodes last for a shorter period, such as less than a week.

Hypomanic episodes are not normally severe enough to seriously disrupt a person's life. In fact, a person can function well during an episode. The problem is, he or she may not recognize that anything is wrong. Without proper treatment, people with BD who experience hypomania can later develop depression or severe mania.

People who show a pattern of hypomanic episodes shifting back and forth with episodes of depression may be diagnosed with bipolar II disorder. People with this form of bipolar disorder experience periods of debilitating depression, but their manic symptoms are less severe than in bipolar I. They never experience full-blown mania or lose contact with reality.

People in a manic state may experience an increased level of grandiosity—a feeling of grand splendor or exaggerated importance. This feeling of grandiosity can also exaggerate feelings of low self-esteem. For example, teens suffering from mania might feel as though they are the worst person in school or the least talented person in music class.

Often, having so much energy can leave people feeling worried or anxious. Mania can also lead to panic attacks, during which the body overreacts and becomes frozen with fear. In extreme cases of mania, people can experience auditory or visual hallucinations. This loss of contact with reality is known as psychosis.

A manic episode can make some people obsessive. They can become overwhelmed with awful thoughts or desires. They can also become compulsive, or feel driven to do something— such as drink, smoke, or eat—by an inner force that seems stronger than their own will. This behavior can be dangerous and can cause people to feel out of control.

For a person's mood to be considered manic, he or she must experience symptoms of mania for most of the day for at least seven days.

Mania Checklist

If you suspect that you, a friend, or a family member might be having a manic episode, consider the list of questions below. Do you or does someone you know:

- Seem to need almost no sleep at all?
- Become easily distracted?
- Feel hyperalert and hypersensitive?
- Fidget and move around constantly?

The family of Sarah Malawista created this traveling art gallery to raise money for arts education. Sarah, a creative teen with BD, committed suicide at age eighteen. Some of her paintings hang outside the bus.

- Act obnoxiously?
- Talk a lot and very quickly?
- Feel on top of the world?
- Become very irritable for no reason?
- Have trouble making decisions?
- Pull dangerous stunts and act invincible?
- Feel full of creative energy?
- Come up with lots of wild and impractical ideas?
- Eat too much, or not at all?
- Drink and do drugs recklessly?

- Spend money excessively?
- Have racing thoughts?

If the answer is yes to four or more of these questions and these symptoms have lasted for more than one week, you might be experiencing a manic episode.

Mood Cycles

Generally, people with bipolar disorder do not swing evenly back and forth from mania to depression. More often than not, the cycles of mania and depression are unpredictable and can last for different lengths of time. One can even experience both at the same time. Some people with BD have extreme cycles only once every few years, although many factors, including stress, can trigger an episode. During periods of emotional stability, the disorder lays dormant and the person is asymptomatic (without symptoms). Psychiatrists call this dormant state euthymia.

Compared to adults, teens with bipolar disorder typically experience faster swings from depression to mania and back again. This process is known as rapid cycling. Rapid-cyclers go through four or more episodes of mania, depression, hypomania, or mixed symptoms within a year. Ultra-rapid cyclers have several episodes within a week, and ultradian cyclers have distinct mood swings within just twenty-four hours.

If your doctor thinks you have bipolar disorder, he or she will attempt to find patterns in your cycling mood swings to help determine your diagnosis and treatment.

A Dangerous Disease

Both the depressive and manic phases of the disease can be dangerous for someone with BD. The depressive phase is often considered more dangerous. When people are in this extremely low, hopeless state, entertaining the idea of suicide is possible, as are suicide attempts. Both teens and adults with bipolar disorder are at risk for suicidal behavior. In fact, according to the Society for Neuroscience, bipolar disorder has a suicide rate of up to 19 percent for those who do not receive proper treatment. This rate is 15 times higher than that of the general population.

The manic phase poses risks, too. During a manic episode, a person might stay awake for days at a time. Although the person feels as if he or she is bursting with energy, the nonstop activity eventually drains the body's reserves, leaving the person weak, exhausted, and possibly dehydrated. With the body's defenses down, the person risks catching an infectious disease that a healthy body can normally resist.

At the same time, a person's sense of judgment is distorted during manic episodes. This can lead to all sorts of excessive behaviors, such as gambling and spending sprees, promiscuous sex, and physical risk taking (speeding in a car, for example). The

The mother of Aaron Zimmerman holds a family photo of her two sons. Aaron, the boy on the left, was fatally injured after climbing a train platform during a manic episode.

results of such activities, including unplanned pregnancies, sexually transmitted diseases, expulsion from school, losing money, getting fired, and getting arrested, can wreck a person's life. These behaviors can also cause alienation from friends and family.

Drug and alcohol abuse is common among people with bipolar disorder. In fact, according to the National Institute of

Mental Health (NIMH), 60 percent of people who are diagnosed with bipolar disorder are also found to have a substance abuse problem. While the reasons for this link are not yet clear, it is possible that people are not aware that the extreme highs and lows they are feeling are the result of a mental health disorder. Instead of seeking treatment, these people may "medicate" themselves with alcohol and illegal drugs in an effort to alleviate the lows of depression or dull the speed and excessiveness of mania.

Seeking help can prevent many of these high-risk behaviors—and consequences—from happening. Bipolar disorder can be treated, and many of those diagnosed with the illness find a suitable treatment and go on to live healthy, stable lives.

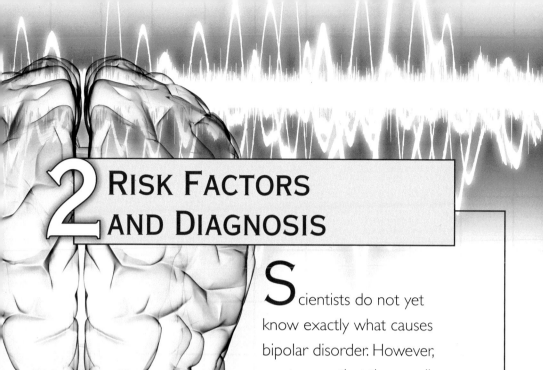

2 RISK FACTORS AND DIAGNOSIS

Scientists do not yet know exactly what causes bipolar disorder. However, most agree that the condition is linked to certain abnormalities in the brain. This is why bipolar disorder is considered a physiological condition and not simply a psychological illness. Scientists believe a combination of four major factors makes people vulnerable to bipolar disorder. These factors are heredity (genes), abnormal brain structure and function, environmental factors, and psychological factors.

Heredity

Bipolar disorder is a hereditary disease, meaning that it runs in the family. Scientists believe that people inherit a combination of genes that make them susceptible to the disorder. Researchers are working to identify all of these genes.

If there is a history of bipolar disorder in your family, this can increase your chance of developing the condition. According to NIMH, people who have a parent or sibling with bipolar disorder are four to six times more likely to get the disease than people in the general population.

Similarly, studies of identical twins show that the twin of a person with BD has a high risk of developing the illness in the future. However, not all people who have an identical twin with BD will develop the disorder. Since identical twins share all of the same genes, these results suggest that genes are not the only factor involved in developing the disease. In addition, many people with BD come from families with no history of bipolar disorder.

Abnormal Brain Structure and Function

Using the latest brain imaging technologies, scientists have discovered that the brain structure and function of people with BD differs from that of people without the illness. According to NIMH, MRI images have shown a decrease in the size of the amygdala and prefrontal cortex in individuals with BD. These brain structures are involved in the processing of emotions. Other kinds of imaging have shown abnormalities in the way

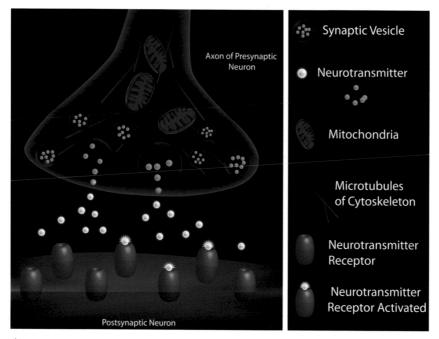

Communication between neurons takes place through the movement of neurotransmitters across a gap called a synapse. Many medications for BD affect this process, bringing about mood changes.

these brain structures work in people with BD. For example, researchers have found reduced activity in the prefrontal cortex during the depressive stage.

Scientists believe that the neurotransmitter system is also linked to bipolar disorder. The brain produces and uses chemicals called neurotransmitters, which are chemical substances that send messages from one nerve cell, or neuron, to another.

People experiencing mania usually have too many neurotransmitters being produced, whereas people in a depressed cycle often have too few. Such excesses or deficiencies upset the communication between the brain and the body. Although scientists still have a great deal to learn about neurotransmitters, once a mood disorder is detected, doctors are often able to correct imbalances with the use of medicine.

Environmental Factors

Your environment is made up of the things you do, the people with whom you interact, and the spaces you inhabit. Some aspects of your environment may make you feel overwhelmed and anxious. It might be that a bully at school always picks on you, that a close friend or relative has died, or that your parents fight a lot. Financial troubles at home, mental or physical illness, and divorce in the family are other events that can leave you feeling unhappy.

When you are under pressure, the body tries to help by producing certain hormones. When you are anxious or afraid, the body can produce excess amounts of a stress hormone called cortisol. Many depressed people often have higher-than-normal levels of cortisol. Scientists think that these high levels may have a damaging effect on the brain and the nerve cells. They are researching whether the changes that result can lead to mood disorders.

Stress from traumatic experiences, such as abuse, divorce, or a death in the family, may trigger a bipolar episode in an individual who is vulnerable to the illness.

Psychological Factors

Regardless of biochemical and genetic factors, your attitude can influence the way that a mood disorder affects you. If you tend to look at things negatively, lack self-confidence, are anxious, and find it difficult to talk about your problems, you will be less able to deal with the mood swings you are experiencing. You also have a stronger chance of becoming depressed.

People who have had a difficult childhood or other challenging life experiences might be more susceptible to mood disorders. Tense family situations, major illnesses, troubles in school, and frequent moving from town to town can make you feel insecure and uncertain about your future. Chronic stress and anxiety can bring on bipolar episodes and make coping with BD difficult.

Onset of the Disease

Anyone, including children and teens, can develop bipolar disorder. However, the illness usually appears during the late teen years or early adult years. The illness then continues throughout a person's life.

Males and females are equally likely to experience bipolar disorder, but it is diagnosed more often in girls. This may be because girls find it easier to talk about their feelings and admit feeling depressed than boys do.

When the illness first appears, both the manic and depressive phases might be mild. In many instances, however, bipolar disorder is first experienced as a depressive episode with all the hallmarks of typical (unipolar) depression. The bipolar symptoms become more severe as time goes on. This is especially true if treatment is not sought early.

Because the symptoms of bipolar disorder may not be obvious, both you and those around you—even your doctor—might blame something else for your extreme moods. Many times, people with BD are at first diagnosed with depression only.

Also, when teens experience a milder manic phase—full of happiness, energy, and confidence— they and others rarely think that anything is wrong. When you are manic, you often feel invincible. Even if you are exhibiting classic symptoms of mania—feeling extremely uninhibited and excited—you likely won't believe you have a problem. Adults may also believe that it is normal for teens to act up, behave unpredictably, and experience mood swings. These factors often delay a diagnosis.

The onset of mania can cause a teen to behave in risky ways. He may believe he can do anything without getting hurt.

Unfortunately, many parents and teachers mistakenly view teens' bipolar disorder symptoms as merely bad behavior. They end up punishing teens instead of looking for the causes of such behavior. If you aren't

Professionals Who Can Help

You can turn to several different professionals for advice and treatment for BD or other mental illnesses. Professional help can come from a psychiatrist, professional therapist, or counselor. Professionals' licenses vary from state to state. A person's credentials can indicate postgraduate continuing education and other criteria required by the state. The following list describes clinicians' areas of expertise and ways in which they can help:

- **General physicians (M.D.):** Medical doctors can diagnose your condition and refer you to a specialist. They can prescribe medication, but do not have specific mental health training or specialization.
- **Psychiatrists (M.D.):** These medical doctors specialize in mental health and have had specific mental health training. They can evaluate and diagnose you and provide medication and therapy.
- **Ph.D. (doctor of philosophy) and Psy.D. (doctor of psychology):** These professionals, also referred to as psychologists and clinical psychologists, have had four to six years of graduate study. They frequently work in schools, businesses, mental health centers, and hospitals where they provide mental health counseling. They may also work in private individual and group practices.
- **M.A. (master of arts degree in psychology):** This is a counseling degree. Many M.A.s have private practices and counsel individuals and families.

- **Ed.D. (doctor of education):** This degree indicates that an individual has a background in education, child development, and general psychology.
- **M.S.W. (master of social work):** This degree prepares an individual to diagnose and treat psychological problems and provide mental health referrals. Psychiatric social workers constitute the single largest group of mental health professionals. Many M.S.W.s have private practices and are on preferred provider lists with insurance companies.

comfortable talking to your parents about your symptoms, try opening up to another adult you trust: an aunt or uncle, a teacher, a coach, a close friend's parent, a clergy member, a school guidance counselor, or a social worker. If the feelings are overwhelming and don't go away, you will need professional help from a psychiatrist, counselor, or therapist.

Diagnosing Bipolar Disorder

Although bipolar disorder is a biological disease, there are no laboratory tests or other procedures that can detect it. Instead, a physician makes a diagnosis based on the presence of a combination of symptoms and risk factors. To do this, he or she will talk to you and your parents to compile a detailed medical history, including your symptoms, both past and present. Doctors focus closely on the symptoms that made you aware that you might be at risk for the condition. They may also focus on the following areas:

- **Development:** Did you have an easy birth? Were you a healthy baby who had no problems learning to walk or talk?
- **Physical health:** Were you a healthy child? Did you have any illnesses, accidents, surgery, or medical conditions?
- **Psychological health:** As a child, were you relaxed or anxious, shy or aggressive? Did you act up?
- **Education:** Have you always done well in school or have you had difficulty? Do you have trouble paying attention in class?
- **Family:** How do you get along with your parents and siblings? Are there any cases of mood disorders, learning disabilities, or alcoholism in your family?

Then, the doctor will give you a physical examination. He or she may order tests, such as blood tests, urine tests, a brain scan, or an electrocardiogram, in order to rule out other medical reasons for your symptoms. For example, the doctor may want to rule out a stroke, brain tumor, or another condition.

According to the *DSM-IV*, to be diagnosed with bipolar disorder, you need to have had at least one manic-depressive episode for a period of at least two weeks. (The *DSM-IV* is the *Statistical Manual of Mental Disorders, Fourth Edition*. It is the standard classification of mental disorders, used by a wide variety of mental health professionals throughout the

MYTHS AND FACTS

Myth: If you have repeated mood swings from depressed to happy, it means that you have bipolar disorder.

Fact: It is quite possible that your moods are ordinary growing pains or symptoms of a different condition. However, children and teens can develop BD, and any severe mood changes should be taken seriously. You and your parents should discuss any questions with a medical professional, preferably a family physician who can give you a complete physical examination and refer you to a psychiatrist or psychologist if necessary.

Myth: If you take medication for bipolar disorder for several months and then feel better, you can stop taking it.

Fact: You must continue to take your medication as your doctor prescribed it, even if you feel better. Deciding on your own to eliminate prescription drugs is dangerous, and abruptly stopping any medication can cause unwanted side effects. In teens with BD, suddenly stopping a medication may lead to "rebound," or a worsening of bipolar disorder symptoms. Always work with your doctor to decide upon any changes in your treatment.

MYTHS AND FACTS *(CONTINUED)*

Myth: If your parent struggles with mania and depression, you will too.

Fact: Just because you have a parent with bipolar disorder, it does not mean that you will develop the illness. Still, your chances of developing the disorder are about four to six times greater than average. Only a mental health professional is qualified to make an assessment of your symptoms. If you feel depressed for more than two weeks and you have lost interest in things that used to appeal to you, consider seeing your family physician for a checkup and psychiatric referral.

United States.)

Often, you are the person best equipped to discover that something is wrong. If your extreme moods are beginning to interfere with your daily life, start keeping a daily journal or mood chart. Record how you are feeling each day. This information can be very helpful to a doctor making a diagnosis. Bipolar disorder is a serious illness, but the sooner a proper diagnosis is made, the sooner you can get help.

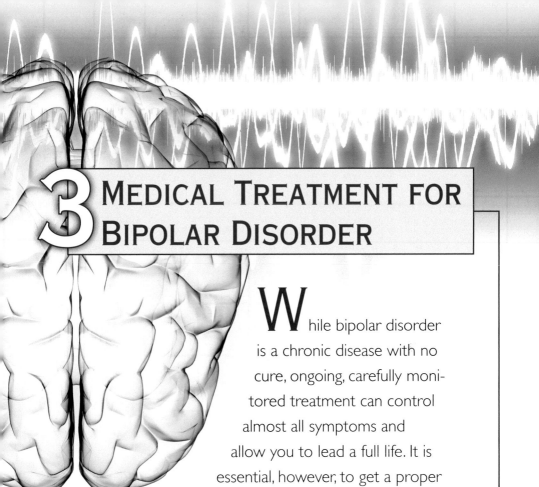

3 MEDICAL TREATMENT FOR BIPOLAR DISORDER

While bipolar disorder is a chronic disease with no cure, ongoing, carefully monitored treatment can control almost all symptoms and allow you to lead a full life. It is essential, however, to get a proper diagnosis. Early detection is important. With bipolar disorder, the earlier you begin treatment, the better your chances are of sustaining meaningful control over your extreme emotional periods.

There are two stages involved in treating bipolar disorder: acute and preventive. Acute-stage treatment aims to control and end temporary manic, hypomanic, depressive, or mixed episodes. Once the episodes are under control, preventive-stage treatment aims to keep them from happening again. Preventive-stage treatment is long-term and ongoing. During both of these stages, treatment consists of three parts:

- **Medications:** Prescription drugs that can control both manic and depressive symptoms
- **Psychotherapy:** Counseling that helps you and your family deal with the problematic feelings and behavior caused by bipolar disorder
- **Education:** Opportunities for you and your family to learn about bipolar disorder and the ways to cope with it

This chapter focuses on the different medications and medical treatments that doctors (professionals such as psychiatrists and general physicians with an M.D.) prescribe for bipolar disorder.

Taking Medication for Bipolar Disorder

Prescription medication for bipolar disorder is usually taken daily at specific times and in specific doses. It is extremely important to take your medication as prescribed. Unfortunately, some people begin skipping doses. Others stop taking medications because they go for a long time without experiencing their symptoms or because, in the midst of a manic episode, they feel invincible or distracted. Sometimes people stop taking their medications because of side effects, such as drowsiness or indigestion. If you find yourself experiencing unwanted side effects, you should talk to your doctor.

Regardless of the reason, if you suddenly stop taking medications—or take them at the wrong time or in the wrong quantities—you can hurt yourself. It can be dangerous or even life threatening if you don't take your medications as directed. Not only can it trigger more severe episodes of mania or depression, it can also have a negative impact on your nervous system.

For the same reasons, you should never mix medication with any other drugs or with alcohol. In addition, you should inform your doctor of all prescription drugs, over-the-counter medications, and supplements you are taking to avoid dangerous effects from mixing certain substances.

There are three important types of medication used to treat bipolar disorder: mood stabilizers, antidepressants, and antipsychotic drugs.

Mood-Stabilizing Medications

Mood-stabilizing medications provide relief from symptoms of severe mania. They also help prevent manic and depressive episodes from recurring (coming back).

One of the oldest and most commonly used mood stabilizers is a natural element called lithium. Lithium (also known by the brand names Eskalith, Lithobid, and Lithonate) works especially well for people who experience pure manic episodes. When it is taken with other medication, it is also effective against depression. However, the trouble with lithium is that too much can be toxic, and too little can prove ineffective.

Mood-stabilizing drugs can even out the extreme moods of people with bipolar disorder. A drug might be used to treat a single pole or to treat both mania and depression.

To make sure the dosage is not harmful, a patient taking lithium needs to have regular blood tests. The quantity of lithium one can take also depends on the side effects it produces. These may include gastrointestinal problems, weight gain, tremors, and fatigue. Luckily, there are other medications that people can take to diminish these side effects.

Another mood stabilizer that works well for many different kinds of manic episodes is valproic acid or divalproex sodium. It is sold under the brand names of Divalproex, Depakote, and

Depakene. Valproic acid acts on the body quickly to improve the transmission of information between neurons. Specifically, it acts on the neurotransmitter gamma amino butyric acid (GABA), which balances brain circuits. Like lithium, valproic acid decreases the severity and frequency of manic episodes, but it is less effective for treating depression.

Valproic acid levels have to be monitored, and people taking the drug should watch for symptoms of possible liver damage such as unusual bleeding or bruising, jaundice (yellowing of the eyes and skin), fever, and water retention.

Other mood-stabilizing medications include lamotrigine (Lamictal), which has been especially useful against depression; gabapentin (Neurontin), which reduces anxiety; and topiramate (Topomax), which works well against mania.

Although these medications may be taken on their own, they are most often combined with each other or with other medications. It is important to note that all of these medications can have side effects such as fatigue, dizziness, and memory loss. These medications also have an FDA warning, which states that they may increase the risk of suicidal thoughts and behaviors. Patients taking these drugs need to be carefully monitored for such side effects. Patients taking these medicines for BD should not make any changes to their medications without consulting their doctors.

In addition, recent studies have indicated that mood stabilizers containing valproic acid may cause hormonal problems in teen girls. According to NIMH, valproic acid can increase levels of testosterone, or male hormone, in young women under age twenty, leading to polycystic ovary syndrome (PCOS). PCOS can cause a young woman's eggs to develop into cysts, or fluid-filled sacs, as well as other serious symptoms. For this reason, doctors do not often prescribe valproic acid to teen girls. When they do prescribe it, they carefully monitor their patients.

Antidepressant Medications

Doctors sometimes prescribe antidepressant medications to help alleviate the symptoms of depression in bipolar disorder. However, on their own, antidepressants can trigger a manic state or rapid cycling in a person with BD. Therefore, doctors usually require patients with BD to take a mood stabilizer at the same time.

Some of the most commonly prescribed antidepressants for BD include fluoxetine (Prozac), sertraline (Zoloft), bupro-pion (Wellbutrin), and paroxetine (Paxil). Generally, antidepressants enable more of the necessary neurotransmitters—serotonin, dopamine, and norepinephrine—to pool around nerve synapses in the brain. In this way, less of the neurotransmitter is reabsorbed. For instance, antidepressants like fluoxetine (Prozac) increase the level of serotonin in the brain. It is theorized that depressed individuals have less of these chemicals that help steady thoughts and emotions.

These antidepressant and antipsychotic drugs are used to treat bipolar disorder. Patients must work closely with their doctors to find the right drug (or drug combination) and dosage.

If one drug produces side effects such as insomnia, dry mouth, or "sour" stomach, ask your doctor to prescribe another. According to NIMH, in some teens and young adults, antidepressants can make depression worse or cause suicidal thinking or behavior. Any unusual changes in behavior or mood, such as agitation, social withdrawal, or trouble sleeping, should be reported to a doctor immediately. People should be watchful for unintended side effects, particularly in the first few weeks of treatment with an antidepressant.

In addition, some antidepressants work better than others for individuals with various bipolar symptoms. Also, antidepressants often take several weeks before they begin altering brain chemistry. Your doctor may experiment with different drugs in varying combinations until he or she finds the best treatment. This process can take several months in some cases. Patients can find this experience exhausting and aggravating, but it is important to remain hopeful and to keep an open mind about drug therapy.

Antipsychotic Medications

Bipolar individuals with unusually strong manic symptoms may become psychotic, or lose touch with reality. Symptoms of psychosis include hearing voices, seeing things that aren't there, feeling paranoid, and believing that one is being followed or stalked. Because weeks can pass before mood stabilizers begin to take effect, doctors sometimes prescribe antipsychotic medication to individuals with bipolar disorder. An antipsychotic drug can quickly stop racing thoughts, pressured speech, and the overactivity associated with mania. Doctors prescribe antipsychotics as needed, sometimes on a short-term basis.

Antipsychotics were developed in the 1930s when scientists began experimenting with a group of chemical compounds called phenothiazines. Many of the compounds had sedative

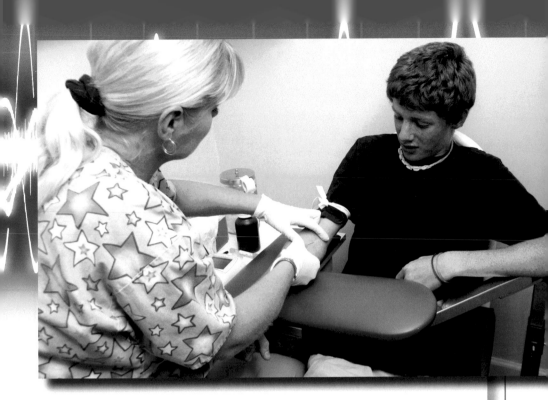

Treatment with some drugs requires regular doctor visits and blood tests to monitor the medication's effects on the body.

properties and were later discovered to be useful during surgical procedures. One drug in this group, chlorpromazine (thorazine), was then used to treat schizophrenic patients. Doctors found that chlorpromazine not only helped to calm patients, but also reduced their hallucinations and delusions.

Today, researchers have developed antipsychotic medications such as olanzapine (Zyprexa), quetiapine (Seroquel), risperidone (Risperdal), and aripiprazole (Abilify). These drugs have similar benefits, but some have fewer side effects than

Electroconvulsive Therapy (ECT)

Electroconvulsive therapy (ECT) can be an effective treatment for patients who suffer from severe mania and depression but have not improved with other treatments.

Cinematic images of past electroconvulsive therapy (ECT) are often horrifying, but today's treatments are much more humane. Today, doctors use anesthetic drugs to temporarily put patients to sleep while the sixty-second ECT treatment is administered. Doctors also administer muscle relaxants to control a patient's muscle spasms. Scientists have discovered that if they stimulate only half of the brain (either the right or left hemisphere), patients will recover more rapidly and will suffer fewer side effects, such as memory loss.

After the initial pulse of electricity is administered (in controlled doses and within timed limits), a patient's right- or left-brain hemisphere sends the body into an induced seizure that lasts roughly forty-five seconds. After approximately five to fifteen minutes, the patient recovers. He or she may feel slightly groggy, woozy, or confused. This reaction is normal and disappears within hours. ECT's long-term side effects seem to center on the brain's memory capacity. About two-thirds of ECT patients have reported some degree of permanent memory loss. Others suffer from retrograde amnesia, or temporary memory loss.

Doctors consider ECT a highly effective treatment for severe depressive, manic, and mixed episodes. A patient is a candidate for ECT treatment if he or she is suicidal, severely depressed but unable to take antidepressant drugs, or unresponsive to drug treatments. ECT is also recommended for pregnant women suffering from bipolar symptoms, who are unable to risk the side effects of drugs.

others. If you are taking any of these drugs, your doctor may request frequent blood tests to monitor your health.

The side effects of antipsychotic medications can include dizziness, sleepiness, rapid heartbeat, and blurred vision. Antipsychotics may also cause weight gain and change a person's metabolism. In rare cases, long-term use of antipsychotic drugs induces a condition called tardive dyskinesia (TD). This condition causes repetitive, involuntary movement of the facial muscles. A person with TD looks as if he or she is chewing, blinking, or sporadically moving his or her lips. Some patients recover after they stop taking antipsychotic medication, but others cannot be cured.

Other Medications for Bipolar Disorder

Doctors may recommend other medications to treat bipolar disorder, depending on the severity of the patient's symptoms. Some of these drugs seem to have beneficial effects for mild forms of bipolar disorder, such as hypomania.

Patients are sometimes given a prescription for a benzodiazepine, a sedative that combats anxiety and stress. Short-term use of a drug in the benzodiazepine family can sometimes calm mania, especially when used in conjunction with antipsychotic medications. Benzodiazepines are controlled substances and should be utilized with care. They can be addictive. Withdrawal symptoms may include seizures, so if you or your family members have a history of seizure disorders, this is not a drug option for you.

Doctors can also prescribe stimulants to BD patients suffering from severe depression, but since the advent of antidepressants in the mid-1980s, they tend to do so less and less. Stimulants such as amphetamines can boost energy levels as well as increase concentration and elevate mood, but they are also quite addictive. They raise blood pressure and increase the potential for heart problems.

Thyroid medications can also alter the moods of people with bipolar disorder. A common treatment to help bipolar patients is the proper regulation of the thyroid gland. For years, doctors have observed a correlation between thyroid hormones and mood. For instance, cycles of depression can intensify in a female just before and during her menstrual cycle when hormones are at their highest monthly level. Other studies indicate that hypothyroidism (abnormally low thyroid functioning) is very common in bipolar patients who experience rapid cycling. For this reason, doctors test patients for thyroid conditions before beginning any drug treatment for depression.

Patients should be on the lookout for the symptoms of thyroid dysfunction. Hypothyroidism can cause weight gain and sluggish or slow behavior. Overactive thyroid functioning, or hyperthyroidism, can cause a rapid pulse rate, an increase in nervous energy, and feelings of anxiety, tension, and undue

10 GREAT QUESTIONS
TO ASK A DOCTOR

Below are just a few of the questions that you should consider discussing with your psychiatrist, psychologist, physician, or other health professional.

1. What type of bipolar disorder do I have, and how severe is it?

2. How can we be certain that I am exhibiting symptoms of mania? Could I just have an excitable personality or attention deficit/hyperactivity disorder (ADHD)?

3. Does bipolar disorder change with age? Is it possible to outgrow it?

4. Can I go off the medication I am taking if I feel that it isn't right for me or if there are unwanted side effects?

5. My mother says that anyone who has bipolar disorder should avoid taking drugs and drinking alcohol, even in moderation. Is that true?

6. I've heard that natural herbs and supplements work well to curb the lows of depression. Can I just take herbs instead of medication?

7. What kinds of changes in behavior should I—or my family members—alert you about?

8. What should I do if I need emergency help during a mood episode?

9. Nobody in my family has depression or bipolar disorder. Why do I have it?

10. If I have bipolar disorder, what are the chances of passing the condition on to my children?

stress. If you are found to have either hypo- or hyperthyroidism, your doctor can prescribe medications to boost or lower the body's level of hormones.

Treating bipolar disorder can be very complicated. What works for one person might not work for another. Also, some drugs might become less effective over time or produce unpleasant side effects. The best results often come from combinations of medications. These combinations are known as medication (med) cocktails. Though med cocktails can be successful, you might still experience occasional episodes of mania or depression. Furthermore, it can take weeks or even months before some drugs take full effect.

4 MANAGING BIPOLAR DISORDER

Initially, any diagnosis of mental illness is difficult to absorb. Many teens and adults go through periods of fear, anger, denial, or even indifference. At first, the diagnosis of bipolar disorder may seem overwhelming. Soon, however, you and your health care professionals will come up with a treatment plan that provides stability. In addition to taking medications, successfully managing BD involves therapy, self-care and self-monitoring, education about the disease, and support from family and friends.

Participating in Psychotherapy

Seeing a psychiatrist, psychotherapist, or another mental health specialist is an essential part of treating bipolar disorder. Psychotherapy, or talk therapy, helps you to understand the disease and

Along with medication, psychotherapy is important for keeping a person's moods in check and changing negative thought patterns and behaviors.

learn how to cope with the feelings and behaviors it can produce. There are four main types of therapy that can help treat bipolar disorder:

- **Cognitive behavioral therapy (CBT)** helps people change harmful behaviors and ways of thinking that can increase or decrease stress and depression.
- **Interpersonal therapy** focuses on how to improve your relationships with those around you.
- **Social rhythms therapy** focuses on how to organize and stick to a daily routine that stabilizes your body's rhythms.
- **Family-focused therapy** includes family members, helping them to recognize new bipolar episodes and teaching them how to help their relative with BD.

You can participate in all of these types of therapy individually or in a group. It is important that you trust and feel comfortable with your therapist. If, after several sessions, you feel it's not working, look for someone else. However, don't give up on therapy altogether.

Students at Columbia College Chicago model the look of depression in an emotional wellness program that uses dance therapy to explore mental illness and suicide.

Practicing Self-Care

An important part of living with bipolar disorder is taking good care of yourself. Although professionals, friends, and family can help, you are the one who can best take steps to make things easier for yourself. The following are some self-care tips:

- **Follow a normal sleep schedule.** Research has shown that an interruption in normal sleep patterns has the potential to trigger manic episodes.
- **Do not use alcohol, drugs, or caffeine.** Other than medications, any substance that interferes with the

body's natural cycles, or acts as a stimulant or depressant, could trigger manic or depressive episodes.

- **Listen to your body.** Learn to watch for the typical early warning signs of an oncoming manic or depressive episode. For example, you might have increasing insomnia if you are about to experience a manic episode or a steady period of lethargy if you are heading into a depressive episode.

A healthy body can have a big impact on a healthy mind. Eat balanced, nutritious meals at least three times a day. Avoid alcohol, caffeine, and junk food because they contain sugar, salt, and artificial ingredients, including chemicals that can disrupt your body's balance. It is also a good idea to drink plenty of water, which helps to prevent dehydration (this is sometimes a side effect of bipolar medications).

Exercise is also important because it helps to release stress and tension. When you exercise, you feel better because the brain naturally releases more neurotransmitters into your brain synapses. Exercise can give you a jump start when you are feeling unmotivated and provide you with a healthy outlet if you are manic. Choose an activity that you can make a regular part of your life.

Stress and tension can aggravate or set off episodes of mania or depression. Therefore, aside from medication and therapy, it is very important to learn to relax. Relaxing takes some practice and concentration. It often involves learning breathing techniques and other ways in which to manage stress.

Creativity and Bipolar Disorder

Vincent van Gogh, the late-nineteenth-century Dutch painter, suffered from bipolar disorder and experienced severe mood swings. It is documented that he sliced off his ear during a fit of despair. This extreme act was probably a result of his condition. When van Gogh was depressed, he felt like an outcast and a failure. He began painting after he was unable to succeed at any other career. He created some of his finest work when he was in the midst of mania. During one seventy-day period in France, he completed seventy paintings—one a day!

Like van Gogh, many great artists have found outlets for their extreme feelings and heightened perceptions through art. The novelists Mark Twain and Virginia Woolf, the poets Lord Byron and Edgar Allan Poe, the artist Michelangelo, the playwright Tennessee Williams, and the composer Robert Schumann all likely suffered from bipolar disorder. This is not just a coincidence. Scientists strongly believe that there is a link between creativity and manic depression. Recent studies indicate that during manic episodes, people tend to have a high creative output.

Many creative geniuses, including Vincent van Gogh, are believed to have had bipolar disorder.

Some people find that exercise, such as yoga or running, helps promote periods of relaxation more easily.

Getting Help from Family and Friends

If you have bipolar disorder, it is a good idea to seek support from friends and family. They are there to help. Communicate calmly and speak clearly about what you are going through.

Family members need to understand bipolar disorder. They also need to remember that a person diagnosed with bipolar disorder does not have control over his or her moods. Unlike people who can exert power over their emotions, people who suffer with mood disorders cannot always restrain reactions that may seem inappropriate or unwarranted. They cannot "snap out of it," or "pull themselves together."

Family members should be careful not to criticize, and they need to remember that medications require time to work efficiently. In general, friends and family need to have patience, speak in clear and uncritical language, and be objective about their interpretation of symptoms. Every late-night cramming session is not the beginning of mania, and sleeping in on a Sunday morning is not necessarily a sign of depression. Family members need to offer support, while understanding that mood disorders can be managed.

However, family and friends should never ignore comments that suggest the person with BD has the urge to hurt himself

Madisen Bigley (right), who was diagnosed with bipolar disorder at age fifteen, shares a laugh with her mother, Marlene Lerner-Bigley (left). Strong family support can help a person with BD stay well.

or herself in any way. Such comments should be reported to a doctor or therapist right away.

The more you and your family know about bipolar disorder, the easier it is to deal with. Be sure to educate yourself about the disorder. Learn everything you can about the disease and ways of treating it. Read books and information on Web sites and join your local chapter of the Depression and Bipolar Support Alliance (DBSA). Ask questions to find out how others deal with bipolar disorder. In this way, an individual can come to terms with the disorder, find the right treatment, and live a happy, productive, and emotionally stable life.

Glossary

antidepressant Medication prescribed to relieve depression. Three of the most common antidepressants are Zoloft, Paxil, and Prozac.

bipolar disorder A mental illness in which emotions swing between two opposite emotional states—depression and mania. It is also known as manic-depressive illness.

compulsive Having a strong, usually irresistible drive to perform a particular action.

correlation A mutual relationship between two or more things.

depression A psychological state in which one feels excessively sad, dejected, hopeless, and withdrawn.

elated Full of high spirits; giddy.

electrocardiogram A medical procedure that shows the changes of electric potential that occur during a heartbeat.

euphoria A feeling of great happiness and excitement, especially one that is exaggerated or inappropriate to a person's life situation.

genetic Relating to genes; something that is hereditary.

hormone A substance made in the body that produces a specific and often stimulating effect on cells.

hyperactivity A state of being excessively active, energetic, and unable to concentrate.

hypomania A mild form of manic depression in which manic phases are less extreme.

invincible Impossible to defeat, subdue, or overcome.

lithium A natural substance commonly prescribed as a mood stabilizer for manic depression.

mania A psychological state in which one feels excessive energy, happiness, and enthusiasm.

neuron A cell that carries messages between the brain and other parts of the body and is the basic unit of the nervous system; nerve cell.

neurotransmitter A chemical in the body that carries a signal from one neuron to another.

obsessive Focused excessively on a single thing, person, activity, or idea.

onset The beginning of a disease.

physiological Relating to the workings of the physical body.

psychological Relating to the workings of the mind.

psychosis A mental state characterized by loss of contact with reality (often with hallucinations or delusions) and an inability to think rationally.

psychotherapy Treatment of mental or emotional disorders through psychological analysis.

For More Information

American Psychiatric Association (APA)

1000 Wilson Boulevard, Suite 1825

Arlington, VA 22209

(888) 35-PSYCH [77924]

Web site: http://www.psych.org

The APA is a national society of physicians who specialize in the diagnosis, treatment, prevention, and research of mental illnesses.

Child and Adolescent Bipolar Foundation (CABF)

820 Davis Street, Suite 520

Evanston, IL 60201

(847) 492-8519

Web site: http://www.BDkids.org

The Child and Adolescent Bipolar Foundation improves the lives of families that are raising children and teens living with bipolar disorder and related conditions.

Depression and Bipolar Support Alliance (DBSA)

730 North Franklin Street, Suite 501

Chicago, IL 60610–7224

(800) 826-3632

Web site: http://www.dbsalliance.org

DBSA is the nation's leading patient-directed organization focusing on depression and bipolar disorder. The organization provides up-to-date, scientifically based tools and information written in accessible language.

Mental Health America

2000 N. Beauregard Street, 6th Floor

Alexandria, VA 22311

(800) 969-6642

Web site: http://www.nmha.org

Through advocacy, education, research, and service, this organization works to improve the mental health of all Americans.

Mood Disorders Association of Ontario

36 Eglinton Avenue West, Suite 602

Toronto, ON M4R 1A1

Canada

(888) 486-8236

Web site: http://www.mooddisorders.on.ca

The Mood Disorders Association of Ontario provides free support to people who are living with depression, anxiety, and bipolar disorder and to their families.

National Alliance on Mental Illness (NAMI)

3803 N. Fairfax Drive, Suite 100

Arlington, VA 22203

(703) 524-7600

Web site: http://www.nami.org

NAMI is dedicated to improving the lives of individuals and families affected by mental illness. The NAMI mission includes advocacy, research, support, and education. Its affiliates are in every state and in over 1,100 local communities across the country.

National Institute of Mental Health (NIMH)

6001 Executive Boulevard, Room 8184, MSC 9663

Bethesda, MD 20892-9663

(866) 615-6464

Web site: http://www.nimh.nih.gov

Part of the National Institutes of Health, the mission of NIMH is to transform the understanding and treatment of mental illnesses through research, paving the way for prevention, recovery, and cure.

Organization for Bipolar Affective Disorders Society

1019 - 7th Avenue SW

Calgary, AB T2P 1A8

Canada

(866) 263-7408

Web site: http://www.obad.ca

This organization helps people affected directly or indirectly by bipolar disorder, depression, and anxiety to live better lives.

Web Sites

Due to the changing nature of Internet links, Rosen Publishing has developed an online list of Web sites related to the subject of this book. This site is updated regularly. Please use this link to access the list:

http://www.rosenlinks.com/bdis/bipo

For Further Reading

Albrecht, Ava T., and Charles R. Herrick. *100 Questions and Answers About Bipolar (Manic-Depressive) Disorder*. Sudbury, MA: Jones and Bartlett, 2007.

Blum, Jenna. *The Stormchasers: A Novel*. New York, NY: Dutton, 2010.

Burgess, Wes. *The Bipolar Handbook for Children, Teens, and Families: Real-Life Questions with Up-to-Date Answers*. New York, NY: Avery, 2008.

Federman, Russ, and J. Anderson Thomson. *Facing Bipolar: The Young Adult's Guide to Dealing with Bipolar Disorder*. Oakland, CA: New Harbinger Publications, 2010.

Hunter, David, and Phyllis Livingston. *Youth with Bipolar Disorder: Achieving Stability* (Helping Youth with Mental, Physical, and Social Challenges). Philadelphia, PA: Mason Crest Publishers, 2008.

Jamison, Kay Redfield. *An Unquiet Mind: A Memoir of Moods and Madness*. New York, NY: A. A. Knopf, 1995.

Kiesbye, Stefan. *Bipolar Disorder* (Social Issues Firsthand). Farmington Hills, MI: Greenhaven Press/Gale Cengage Learning, 2010.

Lowe, Chelsea, and Bruce M. Cohen. *Living with Someone Who's Living with Bipolar Disorder: A Practical Guide for Family, Friends, and Coworkers*. San Francisco, CA: Jossey-Bass, 2010.

Marcovitz, Hal. *Bipolar Disorders* (Compact Research). San Diego, CA: ReferencePoint Press, 2009.

Meisel, Abigail. *Investigating Depression and Bipolar Disorder: Real Facts for Real Lives* (Investigating Diseases). Berkeley Heights, NJ: Enslow Publishers, 2011.

Michaels, Rune. *Nobel Genes.* New York, NY: Atheneum Books for Young Readers, 2010.

Miklowitz, David J. *The Bipolar Survival Guide: What You and Your Family Need to Know.* 2nd ed. New York, NY: Guilford Press, 2011.

Scowen, Kate. *My Kind of Sad: What It's Like to Be Young and Depressed.* Toronto, ON, Canada: Annick Press, 2006.

Silverstein, Alvin, Virginia B. Silverstein, and Laura Silverstein Nunn. *The Depression and Bipolar Disorder Update* (Disease Update). Berkeley Heights, NJ: Enslow Publishers, 2009.

Smith, Hilary. *Welcome to the Jungle: Everything You Wanted to Know About Bipolar but Were Too Freaked Out to Ask.* San Francisco, CA: Red Wheel/Weiser, 2010.

Thakkar, Vatsal. *Depression and Bipolar Disorder* (Psychological Disorders). New York, NY: Chelsea House Publishers, 2006.

Index

About the Authors

Basia Leonard is a health educator and author in New York City.

Joann Jovinelly is an editor and award-winning author. She has written many books for young adults on a variety of subjects.

Photo Credits

Cover Mopic/Shutterstock.com; cover (top), multiple interior argus/Shutterstock.com; pp. 3, 7, 14, 21, 28, 29, 33, 42, 47, 52 (background) CLIPAREA/Shutterstock.com; p. 5 Hristo Shindov/Workbook Stock/Getty Images; pp. 9, 25, 41 iStockphoto/Thinkstock.com; p. 11 Rosebud Pictures/Riser/Getty Images; p. 13 Gerard Fritz/Photographer's Choice/Getty Images; p. 16 Lois Raimondo/The Washington Post/Getty Images; p. 19 Emily Harris/Miami Herald/MCT via Getty Images; p. 23 Alila Sao Mai/Shutterstock.com; pp. 27, 48–49 Hemera/Thinkstock.com; pp. 31, 45 YA/Shutterstock.com; p. 36 Jim Dandy/Stock Illustration Source/Getty Images; p. 39 jb Reed/Bloomberg via Getty Images; p. 50 krtphotoslive/Newscom.com; p. 52 Imagno/Hulton Archive/Getty Images; p. 54 © Gregory Urquiaga/Contra Costa Times/ZUMA Press; back cover, multiple interior iDesign/Shutterstock.com.

Designer: Les Kanturek; Editor: Andrea Sclarow; Photo Researcher: Amy Feinberg